# STALKED AND STRANGLED

## DENNIS RADER: THE BTK KILLER

## A TRUE STORY OF BONDAGE, TORTURE, AND MURDER

GW01057495

**Charlie Lark**

# Introduction:

At the end of the twentieth century, over the span of three decades, the story of the BTK Killer was almost the same as the boogey man. A tale told to frighten women and children about an unknown beast who murdered the innocent. The boogey man, however, remains a figment in the imagination of many, while the BTK Killer is real.

Taunting the media and police, the BTK Killer stalked potentially dozens of women and killed 10 people before he was finally caught. Unlike most serial killers, he went through waiting periods between kills, including one period that lasted eight years before he struck again.

"Bind them. Torture them. Kill them." That was what the BTK Killer did, what he bragged about in his letters and poems to the media, and what he fantasized about.

The BTK Killer gained fame and frightened the public through his taunting letters, using grammar so terrible authorities believed it was done on purpose or part of a code. Despite killing his last person in 1991, the BTK Killer wasn't caught until 2005, nearly 15 years later, when his massive ego led to his arrest. One of his taunting letters was sent in on a floppy disk containing metadata that led the authorities to his front door.

In truth, the BTK Killer was in actually a man named Dennis Rader, a church-going family man leading a horrific double life. Rader later claimed he was forced to kill people because he had "a demon" inside him that made him kill, a demon he called "the Minotaur". A portion of the very first letter Rader wrote to the media claimed: "I can't stop it so the monster goes on ... the pressure is great and sometimes he run the game to his liking. Maybe you can stop him. I can't ..."

"Good luck hunting."

# Chapter 1:

# The Early Life Of Dennis Rader

In March of 1945, Dorothea Mae and William Elvin Rader had their first son in Pittsburg, Kansas. Shortly after his birth, the small family moved to Wichita, Kansas where Dennis would be raised with his three younger brothers. While this story may begin as the American dream, it certainly doesn't end that way.

On the surface, Rader seemed to have a normal childhood. He was a member of the Boy Scouts of America and was active in his local church youth group. He was considered an average student although "slightly withdrawn". Those who knew him described him as "normal", "polite" and "well-mannered".

In reality, Rader wasn't "normal" or "polite". He was already working on what would be his infamous nickname, although he likely didn't realize it at the time. He would bind, torture and kill animals.

Rader would later say of himself, "I actually think I may be possessed with demons, I was dropped on my head as a kid".

Realizing that his dark streak wasn't normal, Rader managed to keep his animal murders a secret. He then started fantasizing about tying up and raping girls. He reportedly showed no interest in music and had no sense of humor, but managed to blend in easily enough. He graduated in 1963 from Wichita Heights High School.

During his free time, Rader would peek into the windows of women and watch them change. Later he would break into their houses when they weren't home, steal their underwear, and wear the clothing himself. He created what was essentially a dungeon in his parent's basement which somehow remained unnoticed by the rest of his family. He would tie himself up, nude except for in wearing only the stolen women's underwear, and take selfies using mirrors or cameras with timers.

As a mediocre student with poor grades, Rader tried college but lasted only two semesters. He then enlisted with the Air Force. After four years of active duty and two years on the reserves he received the Air Force Good Conduct Medal, the National Defense Service Medal, and the Small Arms Expert Marksmanship Ribbon.

In May of 1971, Rader married Paula Dietz and moved close to his childhood home. He went to Butler Community College and graduated with a degree in electronics. Still he was unable to find a career. He spent the next few years going through the motions, trying out a series of dead-end jobs that never lasted more than a few months. He found himself going back to college yet again.

Soon, Rader would begin his murders. It must have been something he planned early on, because he went to Wichita State University to study criminal justice. He was taught how to investigate sexual crimes, serial killings, and how to recover evidence from crime scenes.

"The Minotaur" within Rader must have been restless, because just a few months after going back to school, the BTK Killer murdered his first family of victims.

# Chapter 2:

# His First Killings

It was the beginning of 1974 and Rader was jobless. He began what he called "trolling" for women. He would drop his wife off at work, pick a place, and wander around the neighborhood and make observations of women that he found appealing. He would then imagine binding, torturing and finally killing them.

Rader began stalking a young Puerto Rican family, the Oteros, that had recently moved into his neighborhood. He was fascinated with Latina women, claiming he liked their dark hair and eyes. "I guess they just turn me on," Rader later said. Their 11-year-old daughter, Josephine aka "Josie", was apparently enough of a woman for Rader's tastes.

He watched when the Otero family left in the morning, when they came home and what they did during their free time. For weeks, he took notes on their comings and goings. He started preparing, planning and gathering the tools he thought he would need to kill them. He called these tools his "hit kits", and as he refined his needs through murder, his "hit kits" became more refined as well. The kits usually contained guns, cords from window blinds, black electrical tape, knives, screwdrivers, wire cutters, wire, plastic bags, handcuffs and gloves.

Rader knew the family had two cars. Julie Otero drove two of her children, Josie and Joseph Jr. "Joey" to school on weekdays leaving at 8:45 am. He knew Joseph, the father, left for work in his car at 8:00 am.

In January of 1974, on a cold snowy day, Rader's long-held fantasy of taking human life finally came to pass. Rader had been stalking the Otero family but seemed to have missed a very important detail. Rader timed his arrival for 8:20 am, expecting to avoid confronting Joseph, a former boxer. In broad daylight, he cut the phone line outside the house then made his way into the Otero family home through the unlocked back door.

As Rader entered the home, he unexpectedly met four members of the family eating breakfast. Joseph had wrecked his car a few days prior, breaking some ribs in the crash. Rader, shocked to see the former boxer at the breakfast table, claimed he was a wanted man on the run and needed money, food, and a getaway car.

Rader, armed with a gun, quickly managed to gain control of the situation. He had the father of the household, Joseph Otero, lay face down on the living room floor. The family dog started barking because it realized there was an invader in the home. Rader had Joey move the dog outside through the back door. Once the dog was removed, he took the rest of the family into the back bedroom and tied their hands behind their backs with rope. The family told Rader where he could find the keys to the car and told him where they kept their money. At this point, the family believed Rader was going to leave and that they would be safe.

Rader, of course, not wearing a mask, had no plans to let them go. He was 28 at the time and they could identify him to law enforcement. He also had plans for Josie, later claiming she was made for "SBT". This abbreviation stood for "Sparky Big Time". "Sparky" was the nickname Rader had for his penis.

The first member of the family killed by Rader was Joseph Otero. In Rader's confession, he claimed to have placed a plastic bag over Joseph's head and used a cord to tighten it around his neck. Rader remarked, "I had never strangled anyone before, so I really didn't know how much pressure you had to put on a person or how long it would take." Rader was referring to the amount of time it takes for someone to die from strangulation. Wrapping the bag around the head and tightening it with a cord made it so Rader could watch his victims die more slowly.

Immediately after wrapping the bag around Joseph's head, Rader placed a bag over Julie's head. He used the same method of a plastic bag and cord as he did with her husband. However, Joseph ripped the bag open with his teeth and started struggling to save his family. Rader quickly responded by placing a shirt over Joseph's head and then placed an additional bag over the shirt. Joseph, unable to get bite through the shirt, died fighting to save his family.

When Rader returned to Julie, he strangled her with his bare hands, like he had imagined so many times before. Julie passed out, but quickly woke back up, begging Rader to allow her children to live. She had no idea he was there for Josie. Rader's second strangulation attempt worked and Julie died, although Rader later claimed that he took the bags off the children's heads, tricking Julie into thinking that her children would be spared.

Joseph was 38 and Julie was 33 at the time of their murders.

After Julie had breathed her last, Rader moved on to the children using the same method of a plastic bag and cord. 9-year-old Joey was next, and likely was unable to fight as hard as his father had. Rader was also learning quickly and placed a pillowcase over Joey's head first and then covered it with two white plastic bags. Then he tied a blue T-shirt around Joey's head to finish the job. Rader did not want the little boy breaking through the bag like his father had done.

Soon, only Josie was left. Rader was alone with the 11-year-old girl after he had murdered half of her family. He wanted her to die by suffocation through strangulation as he watched her suffer.

He forced Josie into the basement. He pulled out the rope and tied one end onto a drainage pipe hanging from the basement ceiling and tied the other end around her neck and let her hang from the pipe. Rader cut the 115-pound girl's new bra through the front, pulled her cotton panties down to her ankles, and masturbated on her still warm yet lifeless body.

Once Rader finished, he went through the rooms he had been in to remove any evidence of him being there and took a couple items from the home, a radio and Joey's wrist watch. When questioned about why he took the wrist watch and radio, he simply replied, "I don't know." He later explained that he finished cleaning up, took the keys to the car, walked out the front door, and drove away in their car. The only thing Rader left for law enforcement to find was his semen on the girl's legs.

Rader later claimed after he ditched the car he walked to his own car but realized his knife was missing. He claimed to have driven back to the Otero house, parked his car in their garage, and then retrieved the knife from the yard. At the time, he didn't know the Otero family actually consisted of three other children who would soon be arriving home from school.

When 15-year-old Charlie, 14-year-old Daniel and 13-year-old Carmen came home, they discovered half their family dead. The brutal and vicious murders would later haunt law enforcement as they realized there was now a serial killer in Wichita, Kansas. The nation had no idea they were just beginning a 31-year chase.

News reports at the time quoted police as saying the murders may have something to do with the family being Puerto Rican. "I've worked homicides in this city for some 20 years but this is the most bizarre case I've ever seen ... something might have happened in the old country to bring on the incident".

# Chapter 3:

# The Killings Spree Continues

Rader's childhood fantasy of taking life with his bare hands had finally come true. He no longer had to dream about killing people. He could now sit back and remember what it felt like to strangle someone. He could remember watching the light drain from someone's eyes, seeing their last movements, the feel of a lifeless corpse. Unfortunately, Rader's memory would only satisfy that desire for a short time.

Rader spotted 21-year-old Kathryn Bright heading into her home shortly after his first batch of murders and decided he was going to kill her. He thought she looked vulnerable and alone. Little did he know, Kathryn was one of five children and had a close relationship with her family.

On April 4, 1974, just four months after his first killings, he made his decision to move on her. He called her murder "Project Lights Out". Little information on this murder seems to have survived over the years.

He broke into her house and waited for her to come home. He came in through the backdoor and waited near the bedroom. To the surprise of Rader, 19-year-old Kevin Bright was with his sister even though she was normally alone that time of day. "I didn't have any idea she had a brother," Rader later admitted.

Kathryn and Kevin walked in to discover Rader standing in their home, pointing a gun at them. Again, he had no mask and told them the same tale he told the

Otero family, that he was a fugitive on the run and only needed food, money and a car to continue traveling.

Rader had Kevin tie his sister up in the front bedroom. Rader then tied Kevin up to the bedpost in a separate room and went back to Kathryn. However, Rader was only prepared for one person. When Rader went back to Kevin and tried to strangle him with a pair of stockings, Kevin managed to break his binds and attacked Rader. Rader pulled out his gun and shot the teenager in the head. Kevin fell to the ground as blood began to flow from his skull.

"I just did one of those John Wayne things," Rader said later.

After shooting Kevin in the head, Rader walked into the other room and attempted to strangle Kathryn. However, Kathryn would not give in. She fought Rader with all her strength. "She fought like a hellcat," he later said.

Kevin was still alive even though he had just been shot in the head moments earlier. Kevin attacked Rader again and got the gun from Rader's shoulder holster, nearly putting a round in him. Immediately, Rader broke away from Kevin and pulled out his other handgun and shot Kevin a second time assuming the young man was finally dead.

Rader claimed in his confession, "If I would have brought my stuff and used my stuff, Kevin would probably be dead today."

Rader returned to Kathryn with the hope that he would once again experience the "Big G", which is what he called sexual gratification. However, his hope was soon lost. Rader described the murder of Kathryn as a messy encounter that didn't go as planned. Rader said, "went back to finish the job on Kathryn and she was fighting … was basically losing control. Strangulation wasn't working on her. And I used a knife on her."

Rader stabbed Kathryn 11 times, later saying, "well it was a total mess. I didn't have control of it."

Soon after the stabbing, Rader heard noises coming from outside the home. He walked out of the bedroom to find the front door wide open and Kevin running down the street. Kevin survived both gunshots and had escaped from Rader.

In Rader's confession, he said he saw the front door open and thought the cops had entered the home. It was at that moment that he realized he needed to leave. He grabbed the keys to their truck and attempted to drive away. But the truck would not start and Rader was forced to make his escape on foot. He ran down the street to where his car was parked, got in, and made his getaway.

Kathryn was bleeding from the knife wounds but she still would not give up. She crawled through her house to the phone, and when police arrived they found her with the phone in her hands. She eventually died at the hospital from her stab wounds. Kevin survived the attack but was left with permanent damage. He described Rader as, "an average-sized guy, bushy mustache, 'psychotic' eyes".

The failed attempt to kill Kevin combined with the stabbing of Kathryn disappointed Rader. He was not able to receive pleasure from his killing since nothing went as planned. He did not brag about this murder like the other ones, in fact, when he was first caught and named his victims, he left out Kathryn's name. He counted it as a loss and did not want to be recognized for the murder. This was the only murder he later claimed he was ashamed of committing.

When he was caught, 31 years later, they found the Boy Scout knife Rader had used to stab Kathryn with in a cabinet in his kitchen.

# Chapter 4:

## Narcissism And The Title "BTK"

In October of 1974, just six months after killing Kathryn Bright, local media began to talk about the Otero murders again. No one had made a link between the slayings. Three men had turned themselves in after confessing to the murder of the family. This angered Rader and caused him to write a letter to a local news station so he could get the recognition he "deserved".

He began his letter by claiming that the guys who turned themselves in were lying. He was the real killer. He could prove it. He wanted the recognition.

He went on to explain the crime scene of the Otero family in detail and how he murdered the wife, husband, and two children.

His first killings were just enough to make him feel invincible. He stalked the Otero family for weeks before making his move, but while he was stalking, his attraction to Julie and Josie Otero increased. While it was not explicitly mentioned in the televised news broadcasts when their deaths were revealed to the public in 1974, his attraction would be revealed nearly thirty years later in his televised confession.

Rader suffered from a narcissistic personality disorder that made him want to be recognized for his crime. In fact, the name "BTK" came from Rader's desire to be recognized for the Otero killings. When the local news station broadcasted the story, they never mentioned who killed the family. This enraged Rader, which caused him to write a letter to the local news station describing the killings in detail. He wanted Wichita to know the true story so he could receive credit for the killings.

His letter has been copied below. His original letter contained many spelling and grammatical mistakes, which have not been altered or changed. It was originally thought his grammatical errors were a clever way of disguising his writing and personality. Decades later, after Rader was captured, that theory was soundly disproved. It turns out he was actually just not that smart.

Rader wrote:

> I write this letter to you for the sake of the tax payer as well as your time. Those three dude you have in custody are just talking to get publicity for the Otero murders, They know nothing at all. I did it by myself and no ones help. There has been no talk either. Lets put it straight.
>
> Joe:
>
> Position: Southwest bedroom, feet tie to the bed. Head pointed in a southerly direction.
>
> Bondage: Window blind cord.
>
> Garrote: Blind cord, brown belt.
>
> Death: The old bag trick and strangulation with clothes line rope.
>
> Clothed: White sweat shirt, green pants.
>
> Comments: He threw up at one time. Had rib injury from wreck few week before. Laying on coat.
>
> Julie:

Position: Laying on her back crosswise on the bed pointed in southwestern direction. Face cover with a pillow.

Bondage: Blind cord.

Garrote: Clothes line cord tie in a clove-hitch.

Death : Strangulation twice.

Clothes: Blue house coat, black slack, white sock.

Comments: Blood on face from too much pressure on the neck, bed unmade.


Josephine:

Position: Hanging by the neck in the northwest part of the basement. Dryer or freezer north of her body.

Bondage: Hand tie with blind cord. Feet and lower knees, upper knees and waist with clothes line cord. All one length.

Garrote: Rough hemp rope 1/4 dia., noose with four or five turns.

Clothes: Dark bra cut in the middle, sock.

Death: Strangulation once, hung.

Comments: Most of her clothes at the bottom of the stairs, green pants, and panties. Her glasses in the southwest bedroom.


Joseph:

Position: In the east bedroom laying on his back pointed in eastern direction.

Bondage: Blind cord.

Garrote: Three hoods; white T-shirt, white plastic bag, another T-shirt

Clothes line cord with clove-hitch.

Death: Suffocation once, strangulation-suffocation with the old bag trick.

Clothes: Brown pants, yellow-brown stripe T-shirt

Comments: His radio is blaring .

All victims had their hands tie behind their backs. Gags of pillow case material. Slip knots on Joe and Joseph neck to hold leg down or was at one time. Purse contents south of the table. Spilled drink in that area also, kids making lunches. Door shade in red chair in the living room. Otero's watch missing. I needed one so I took it. Runs good. Thermostat turn down. Car was dirty inside, out of gas.

I'm sorry this happen to society. They are the ones who suffer the most . It is hard to control myself. You probably call me 'psychotic with sexual perversion hang-up.' When this monster enter my brain I will never know. But, it here to stay. How does one cure himself? If you ask for help, that you have killed four people they will laugh or hit the panic button and call the cops.

I can't stop it so the monster goes on, and hurt me as well as society. Society can be thankful that there are ways for people like me to relieve myself at time by day dreams of some victims being torture and being mine. I a big complicated game my friend of the monster play putting victims number down, follow them, checking up on them, waiting in the dark, waiting, waiting. . . the pressure is great and sometimes he run the game his liking. Maybe you can stop him. I can't. He has already chosen his next victim or victims. I don't know who they are yet. The next day after I read the paper, I will know, but it to late, Good luck with your hunting.

YOURS, TRULY GUILTILY.

P.S. Since sex criminals do not change their M.O. or by nature cannot do so, I will not change mine. The code words for me will be ... Bind them, Torture them, Kill them, B.T.K., you see be at it again. They will be on the next victim.

Law enforcement were now able to identify his killings and could say with certainty that there was a serial killer on the loose in Wichita, Kansas. The local cops had never had such a thing in their city. Bar fights and spousal killings, yes, but nothing like the Otero family and Kathryn Bright.

The murders committed by Rader in 1974 would haunt law enforcement for more than thirty years. Though they were on the hunt for the killer, they had no solid leads and no way of finding Rader. To make matters worse for law enforcement, the BTK Killer would disappear from Wichita and would not strike again for three years.

# Chapter 5:

## Sexual Stimulation & The "Big G"

For Rader, killing was not only something he wanted to do, it was something that gave him perverse pleasure. Most serial killers find pleasure in the ways in which they choose to kill their victims. The BTK Killer's method of murder was rather unique compared to other serial killers.

The BTK Killer did not rape his female victims like many other serial killers. Rader's sexual fulfillment or "Big G" came from his fantasy of strangling his victims. To him, sexual stimulation came from wrapping a bag around a person's head and watching as they slowly died. His "Big G" did not happen while he was killing, as it is with so many other serial killers, but after his victims had died. He would then pull down his pants and masturbate on his victim's corpses. He would purposely leave semen for investigators to find. To Rader, this was the ultimate fulfillment needed to satisfy his desire.

When the BTK Killer would strangle his victims, he did not always do it with his hands. He preferred to wrap a plastic bag around a person's head and use a cord to seal the bag around their neck. This allowed him to watch his victims die while simultaneously fondling "Sparky". For him, this was his sexual fantasy he had dreamed about his whole life and was finally able to experience it.

He stalked his victims because it was part of the fantasy. While most of his victims were women, the BTK Killer did have two male victims, Joseph Otero and his son, Joey Otero Jr.

In the BTK Killer's confession, he made it seem like his sexual fantasy was only about Josie in the murder of the Otero family. He briefly mentioned the killings of the father and son and made it seem like they were just in his way. However, he made no clear distinction of his preferred gender to fantasize about and may have preferred both genders.

Another strange thing about the BTK Killer's pattern was the amount of time in between his killings. He was not like most serial killers, who killed often and in most cases, faster and faster. When a serial killer starts killing more people, it's more likely they'll make a mistake and get caught. Rader had years in-between his murders, which made it difficult for investigators to track him.

However, the amount of time between the BTK Killer's murders puzzled investigators for a long time. While there are many opinions, it is known that that Rader took pictures of his victims and stole trinkets from their homes. He used them to entertain himself in-between each strangling. Eventually though, the photos and trinkets wouldn't be enough.

In later kills, Rader would play with the bodies after he murdered people. He would strangle them, then position their bodies in the ways he had imagined in his fantasies. He then took pictures so he could reminisce.

His first murders were experiments to see if he could get away with taking lives. After proving he could get away with it, he began killing his victims in more violent and torturous ways.

The BTK Killer would tie his victims up so they could not fight back. They couldn't remove the bag he placed on their head. He eventually learned the exact moment when his victims were about to die. He would strangle them until this point and then he would remove the bag and let them revive. As they came back to life, he would whisper in their ear, "I am the BTK," and start to strangle them again.

The torture was not being tied up and killed. The torture was being tied up and strangled multiple times before the BTK Killer would finally let them die.

Rader loved to exert control and he loved his perception of being invincible. His method of torture allowed him to control life and death, which is why he would strangle his victims over and over again before allowing them to die.

He believed he could kill anyone he wanted, at any given time, and torture them without ever being caught. This made the BTK Killer feel like an invisible "God" who controlled the world around him.

Another peculiar thing Rader did, that was later discovered, were the pictures he had taken of himself during the years he was not killing people. He would tie himself up, place a bag over his head, and take pictures of his body. In one set of pictures, he was dangling from a tree as if he hung himself. In another set, he dug a hole in the ground, tied himself up, placed a bag over his head, and got in the hole as if he was one of his victims.

It is believed that by pretending he was one of his victims it would help him control his urges during his "off years", when he wasn't binding, torturing, and killing people. In later testimonies from his neighbors, they claimed to have seen Rader in the treehouse in his backyard. It is believed that he would go into the treehouse and look at the pictures of himself and his victims while pleasuring himself.

## Chapter 6:

## Hydraulic Street: Shirley Vian

The BTK Killer's next murder victim was a young mother named Shirley Vian. This was three years after Rader had murdered Kathryn Bright. Rader had been stalking an intended victim and planned to kill her on March 17, 1977. He walked up to her front door, knocked, but no one answered.

Pumped up with the urge to kill, the BTK Killer walked down the street and began casing the neighborhood. He found his next victim, Shirley Vian.

The BTK Killer started talking to a boy on the street, showing the boy a picture of Rader's own wife and infant son, asking if he had seen them. 5-year-old Steve answered no and headed home. He had no idea he was leading the BTK Killer right to his house.

Steve would later remember the discussion. "I told him, 'No, sir.' He said, 'Are you sure? Look at it again.' I told him, 'No, sir.' I didn't know who it was."

Rader followed Steve, Shirley's son, home and knocked on the door. Steve excitedly raced one of his brothers to the door, pulled the door open, and Rader just walked in. Steve would talk about letting the BTK Killer into his home decades later and claimed Rader "immediately starts pulling blinds, turns off the TV, reaches in his shoulder holster and pulls out a pistol".

Shirley walked out of her bedroom a moment later and did what she could to save the lives of her three children. Rader told her that he suffered from sexual fantasies and needed to tie her up to receive gratification. She agreed to let him tie her up, believing this would allow her children to live.

Rader and Shirley put the children in the bathroom. He had her put some of the children's toys and blankets in there before he barricaded them in. Rader took her to the bedroom to tie her up. After he had her tied, he pulled out a rope and strangled her to death.

Rader later explained how the killing occurred and described it as a random murder. The following is a record of the words Rader used to describe the death in his confession.

Rader said:

>...she was completely random. There was actually someone across from Dillon's was a potential target. It was called Project Green...I drove to Dillon's and parked in the parking lot and watched this particular residence and then got out of the car...Knocked, nobody answered it.

>So, I was all keyed up. So I just started going through the neighborhood. I had been through the neighborhood before. I kind of knew a little of the layout of the neighborhood. I'd been through the back alleys and knew where certain people lived. While I was walking down Hydraulic, I met a young boy and asked him if he could I.D. some pictures. Kind was a ruse I guess...And I had to feel it out and saw where he went. I went to another address, knocked on the door.

Nobody opened the door. So, I just noticed where he went and went to that house.

After I tried this one residence, nobody came to the door, I went to this house where he had went in, knocked on the door, and told them I was a private detective, showed them a picture that I just showed the boy and asked if they could I.D. the picture. And at that the time, I had the gun here and I just kind of forced myself in. I just walked in...then pulled a pistol.

I told Mrs. Vian that I had a problem with sexual fantasies and I was going to tie her up and may that I might have to tie the kids up. And if she would cooperate with us cooperate with me at that time. We went back. She was extremely nervous. I think she even smoked a cigarette. And we went back to one of the back areas of the porch, explained that I had done this before. And I think she at that point in time, I think she was sick, because she had her night robe on...I think she came out of the bedroom when I went in the house.

So anyway, we went back to her bedroom and I proceeded to tie the kids up and they started crying and got real upset, so I said, "oh, this is not going to work." So, we moved them to the bathroom. She helped me. And then I tied the door shut. We put toys and blankets and odds and ends in there for the kids, to make them as comfortable as we could...we tied one of the bathroom doors shut so they couldn't open it...she went back to help me shove a bed up against the other bathroom door.

And then I proceeded to tie her up. She got sick and threw up. I got her a glass of water, comforted her a little bit and then I went ahead and tied her up and put a bag over her head and strangled her.

I'm sure it was plastic bag...I had tied her legs to the bed post and worked up with the rope all the way up. And then what I had left over, I looped over her neck.

Well, the kids were really banging on the door, hollering, screaming. And then the telephone rang. And they had talked about earlier that the neighbors were going to check on them, so I cleaned everything up real quick-like and got out of there, left and went into my car.

After strangling Shirley Vian, the BTK Killer packed up his things and left the children in the bathroom as he claimed in his confession. The children could see through a bathroom window and knew their mother was being murdered. They escaped through a tiny window in the bathroom. Rader's fear of being captured saved the children's lives even though they had lost their mother.

The BTK Killer planned to kill the children just as he had done with the Otero family. However, the ringing of the phone, combined with the children banging on the door, forced Rader to spare them.

The story of Shirley Vian reveals the cold-hearted nature of Rader's desire to kill and the violence he induced on the world. However, the story Rader explained in his confession was mild compared to the actual event.

He left out some important details including his "Big G" received from the strangling of Shirley. Semen was found at the Otero family scene, but there was nothing at Kathryn Bright's crime scene. For the first time, investigators had evidence to support their idea that these murders were sexually motivated. Rader purposely placed Shirley's panties next to her dead body after he had ejaculated into them. Some detectives who worked the cased believed that Rader was pleasuring himself sexually while Shirley was suffocating from the plastic bag he had tightened around her neck.

Little Steve, all grown up now, still thinks about the last time he saw his mother, "laying face down with a plastic bag over her head, a rope tied around her neck, all the fingers in her hand broken, her hands taped behind her back. That's what I remember".

# Chapter 7:

## "Project Fox Hunt"

In December of 1977, the same year the BTK Killer strangled Shirley, he stalked Nancy Fox and eventually killed her. Even after he had killed Nancy and Shirley, law enforcement did not give Rader the recognition he wanted. The news stations did not recognize him as the killer and the city of Wichita, Kansas was unaware there was a serial killer on the prowl.

The lack of recognition irritated Rader and caused him to write two letters to a news station in hopes that they would talk about him publicly. He had written a letter in 1974, which described the strangulation of the Otero family, and a second letter in 1978 that described the murders of Shirley Vian and Nancy Fox. Attached to this letter was a poem titled, *Oh! Death to Nancy*, which was a reiteration of the poem "Oh Death."

OH! DEATH TO NANCY
What is this taht I can see,
Cold icy hands taking hold of me,
For Death has come, you all can see.
Hell has open it,s gate to trick me.
          Oh! Death, Oh! Death, can't you spare
me, over for another year!

I'll stuff your jaws till you can't talk
I'll blind your leg's till you can't walk
I'll tie your hands till you can't make a
stand.

And finally I'll close your eyes so you
can't see
I'll bring sexual death unto you for me.
B.T.K.


Rader showed his anger with the media for the lack of recognition in his second letter. He made it clear that he strangled Shirley Vian and Nancy Fox and wanted the media to acknowledge the BTK Killer. He began his letter with the shocking statement: "I find the newspaper not writing about the poem on Vain unamusing…How many do I have to Kill before I get a name in the paper or some national attention?"

The BTK Killer had written a poem about the murder of Shirley Vian on a 3x5 index card. The poem was never delivered to the news department. It was received just before Valentine's Day and was sent to the classified ad department. The poem started "Shirley locks, Shirley locks". It was later released to the public.

**SHIRLEY LOCKS! SHIRLEY LOCKS**
**WILT THOU BE MINE?**
**THOU SHALT NOT SCREEM**
**NOR YET FEE THE LINE**
**BUT LAY ON CUSHION**
**AND THINK OF ME AND DEATH**
**AND HOW ITS GOING TO BE.**

The murder of Nancy Fox caused the city of Wichita, Kansas to panic in the wake of the BTK Killer's devastation. Behind him were seven dead bodies and a police chief who refused to announce that a serial killer was on the prowl.

To make matters worse, the thing BTK wanted most was recognition for the murders. He craved the attention and would stop at nothing to get it. The police chief realized the danger of making the announcement, but he had no choice but to tell the public since Rader was going to kill again if he did not get his recognition.

In the book, *Confession of a Serial Killer: The Untold Story of Dennis Rader, the BTK Killer*, Rader's unnerving description of Nancy's death was recorded. The words he used to describe the murder are bone-chilling.

Rader said:

> She came in. She was startled. She asked what I was doing there. After we confronted each other, I told her I traveled a lot, I meant no real harm. I had a sexual problem. I wanted sex. I would tie her up and take a picture. She took her parka off. I believe it was white or cream colored. As she laid [sic] parka down, and began to smoke, I sat on the couch, and she sat in a chair west side of living room [sic]. She was upset.

We talked for a while. I went through her purse, identifying some stuff I'd want to take, and she finally said, "Well, let's get this over with so I can call the police." She sealed her doom for sure when she told me she would contact the police. I wore no mask, or anything to hide my face. I had to kill her.

"Can I go to the bathroom?" she asked me.

I said, "Yes."

She went to the bathroom. I put something in place to block her from closing and locking it and kept an eye on the door, while undressing. I told her when she came out to make sure that she was undressed. She left her sweater on. I started to remove it. She asked me not to, so I didn't. For some reason, she asked that I leave the bedroom door open, which I did. This relates to other times when I respected a victim's request.

I handcuffed her, hands behind her back. I had her lay on the bed, and then I tied her feet and gagged her. I asked if she had ever had sex in the butt with her boyfriend. I had no intention of normal rape sex or even sodomy. I wore no condom at that time, so actually to me it was metal rape or sodomy. That's all I needed with a victim in bondage. The act of strangling brought gratification quickly, along with the victim struggling.

I got on top of her, and then I reached over, took a belt (mine or hers) and then strangled her with it.

[Fox passed out.] I had her come back, and I whispered in her ear a little bit. I told her I was BTK, I was a bad guy … was the torture thing. You can visualize being tied up and knowing that something is going to happen to you, and you can do nothing. That's my torture.

I took the belt off and retied that with pantyhose real tight, removed the handcuffs and tied her hands with pantyhose. I think I might have tied her feet, if I hadn't already tied them, but I think I had. At that time, I masturbated into her blue nightgown. It must have been like with Josephine Otero. I was too sexually excited to hold. Blue, one of my favorite colors, matched with the blue nightgown.

The BTK Killer went on to explain how he went through her dresser drawers and purse as she was dying to get the items he picked out earlier. He took her driver's license and kept it in what he called his "hidey hole". He also took some jewelry, which he thought about giving to his wife and daughter, but decided against it and later remarked that it was "too cruel". Among the treasured belongings of Nancy, he took some lingerie and "...did some sexual things to those later".

The strangling of Nancy Fox was his "most enjoyable" and famous killing. After he left Nancy dead in her apartment, he went to a payphone to make a call. He dialed 911 and told the operator, "You will find a homicide at 843 South Pershing. Nancy Fox." The operator repeated the address and Rader replied, "That is correct."

Then Rader simply walked away leaving the phone dangling from the telephone booth. It was as if he wanted to send the message to the police that he was playing a game with them. Leaving the telephone hanging symbolized his method of strangulation and it demonstrated how he knew he could get away with it.

Many years after Nancy's death, Rader explained how it was the "perfect" murder. His reasoning for calling her death "perfect" was because he had full control of her. He described the feeling of control as the ability to do whatever he wanted to her with no one to stop him. This made him feel powerful. It made him feel like he was an omnipotent and all-powerful "God".

He felt so powerful that he called law enforcement to tell them he murdered Nancy Fox. He did not call just to inform them of her death. He did it because he wanted them to know he was proud of what he did and he believed he deserved recognition. He did it because he wanted to taunt the police.

Shortly after discovering the body of Nancy Fox in her apartment, the police chief made the decision to make the announcement that there was a serial killer on the loose and he had killed seven people so far. He gave Rader the recognition he craved by publicly calling him the "BTK" and making him responsible for the strangling that had occurred in Wichita, Kansas.

At the time the BTK Killer was murdering Nancy Fox, Rader's wife, Paula, was three months pregnant with their second child.

# Chapter 8:

## The One Who Got Away

It was 1978 and the BTK Killer felt that he had gotten quite good at killing. He had a routine. He would stalk someone, learn their comings and goings, and once he thought he knew enough about them he would move in for the kill. Rader believed that the murder of Nancy Fox had been the perfect crime.

The BTK Killer was ready to claim his next victim. His target was Anna Williams, a recent widow.

Rader waited for nightfall and cut Anna's phone line. He then let himself into the house through a basement window. He soon realized Anna wasn't home.

The BTK Killer rummaged through the house while he waited to Anna to arrive. As per usual, he stole trinkets from her home. He always stole trinkets.

He waited and waited. At 10:00 pm Anna still wasn't home. Rader got angry and left.

Anna got home hours after the BTK Killer had left. She knew immediately something was wrong. A door she had left closed was open. She wanted to call the police and picked up the phone, but immediately noticed that there was no dial tone.

Anna ran out of her house to a neighbor and called the police.

When the police arrived at her home, they noticed a wire fashioned in the shape of a noose next to her bed. In a taunting letter sent earlier, the BTK Killer had promised to hang his next victim.

Anna never stayed at the house again. She sent her daughter to get her mail occasionally. A few months later, a package arrived from the BTK Killer. Inside was a pair of pantyhose and a crudely made drawing of what Rader had planned to do to Anna. He also included a poem he wrote for Anna, "Oh Anna Why Didn't You Appear?"

Police later published the poem in the hopes that someone who had seen a draft of it would come forward.

**"Oh Anna Why Didn't You Appear?"**
T' was perfect plan of deviant pleasure so bold on that Spring nite My inner felling hot with propension of a new awakening season

Warn, wet with inner fear and rapture, my pleasure of entanglement, like new vines at night

Oh, Anna, Why Didn't You Appear Drop of fear fresh Spring rain would roll down from your nakedness to scent to lofty fever that burns within, In that small world of longing, fear, rapture, and desparation, the game we play, fall on devil ears Fantasy spring forth, mounts, to storm fury, then winter clam at the end.

Oh, Anna Why Didn't You Appear Alone, now in another time span I lay with sweet enrapture garments across most private thought

Bed of Spring moist grass, clean before the sun, enslaved with control, warm wind scenting the air, sun light sparkle tears in eyes so deep and clear.

Alone again I trod in pass memory of mirrors, and ponder why for number eight was not.

Oh, Anna Why Didn't You Appear


Anna didn't appear because she was out late, square-dancing.

# Chapter 9:

## The BTK Killer Finds Employment In Unlikely Places

Before his first murders, the BTK Killer was bouncing from job to job. After murdering the Otero family, Rader got his first serious job, at ADT Security Services. He kept the position for 14 years, eventually becoming a supervisor.

Through his employment at ADT, the BTK Killer installed home security systems. This job, obviously, gave him insight into the security systems in homes. He also was allowed into hundreds of homes to scout out for potential victims of both stalking and murder. He was able to check out entry and exit points just in case he decided to return later and murder someone.

Additionally, Rader also worked for a time for the United States government working as a temporary census agent. This gave the BTK Killer a legitimate reason to travel all over the state and search people's homes. Once again, he had a job that allowed him easy access in his quest for his choice of victims.

The BTK Killer also was a local "compliance officer". With this job he had a gun, badge, and the ability to intrude into people's lives. He was able to use this position to take classes from law enforcement. These classes taught him even more information on how to clean up his own crime scenes and leave less evidence.

His duties as a compliance officer included "driving around Park City (potentially trolling for victims), observing homes and businesses for compliance with animal control, zoning, beautification (lawn work), broken vehicles, and more". Once more he was able to use his job to find potential victims. He worked as a compliance officer until his arrest.

After his arrest, stories began to come forward about Rader abusing using his position of power as a compliance officer to mistreat others and even going so far as to shoot dogs.

# Chapter 10:

# The Christian Killer

The BTK Killer seemed to have gotten his recognition and vanished from the public. After his botched plans with Anna, there were no more murders claimed by the BTK Killer for almost eight years until the death of Marine Hedge in 1985. However, her murder was slightly different from the rest. She was also one of the oldest victims to be strangled by Rader.

Most people do not consider the personal faith of serial killers when investigating murder scenes. But Dennis Rader stands out since at least one of his victims ended up in the parking lot of his church. His need to feel powerful and desire to be like a God drove him to the point of committing his violent acts inside what he called, "The House of God".

On April 27, 1985, the BTK Killer struck again. This time, he killed one of his neighbors, Marine Hedge, who lived just a few doors down from his house. Rader described her as the woman down the street he would talk to while they were both doing yard work. Other than the average neighborly wave of the hand, Rader and Hedge did not talk much. However, the fact that she lived so close to him gave him the advantage because he could stalk her from his own home. He later remarked that he fantasized about "...what her neck would look like with a rope around it".

Rader knew that he would need an alibi since the murder would take place so close to his home. He knew law enforcement would come knocking on his door for basic questioning after the murder was discovered by police. Rader could not take the chance of becoming a possible suspect in killing.

He had become a leader in the Boy Scouts and was preparing to go on a camping trip with the group. His time in the Scouts taught him how to tie many different knots, which is why investigators found different styled knots in the rope used on his victims. He realized that law enforcement could not accuse him of anything if he was out in the woods camping. He chose to kill Marine on the weekend of his camping trip.

Rader went camping and then somehow snuck away from the group for a couple of hours. He drove his car to a bowling alley near her home to park his car. Once there, he called a taxi cab to come pick him up. He swilled beer around in his mouth and acted drunk to make the cab driver think he was intoxicated. A block or so from his victim's home, Rader made the driver stop by saying he needed some fresh air. Rader got out of the cab, paid the driver, and began walking to Marine Hedge's home.

Once he arrived, he found her car sitting in the driveway even though she was not supposed to be home. He decided to enter the home as a prowler after he had cut the telephone line to the home. Once he was inside the home, he heard the windows rattle, which meant someone was coming in through the front door. To the surprise of Rader, Marine came home with a male friend. Rader waited in the bedroom for nearly an hour until her guest left.

Rader continued to wait until the "wee hours of the morning" to make his final move. He snuck into her bedroom while turning the bathroom light on so he could have clear vision. Turning on the light naturally woke Marine up. It was at this moment she realized there was an intruder in her home. To her surprise, the unmasked man was her neighbor, Dennis Rader.

She started to scream, which caused the BTK Killer to jump on the bed to strangle her immediately. Unlike his other killings, Rader wrapped his bare hands around Marine's neck and squeezed until she died. He didn't use a plastic bag nor did he tie her up as he had previously done with his other victims. In his own words, he "strangled her manually."

After Marine breathed her last, Rader stripped the clothes from her body and tied her up. He placed her on a blanket, went through her personal belongings for trinkets, figured out how to get her out of the house, and then finally moved her to the trunk of her car. He drove the car to Christ Lutheran Church, where he was a member of the congregation. He would later become president of the church.

There he posed her body for his pictures using his polaroid camera. He posed her body at many different angles and in different forms of bondage that would be used to arouse him later.

The BTK Killer put her body back into the trunk of the car after taking his pictures. Rader searched for a place to hide her body and finally found an area with some tree limbs to cover her body. He parked the car on the side of the road and pulled her body out of the trunk. He then placed her body in a ditch where he covered her body with brush and tree limbs.

Marine Hedge's body was found days after Rader had strangled her in her bedroom. One of her co-workers was concerned when Marine did not show up to work. This made law enforcement look for her whereabouts. However, her car was found in the parking lot of a shopping center where Rader had left it.

He cleaned his fingerprints so no trace of his involvement could be found. Later her purse was found on the side of the road and her body was discovered shortly after.

Law enforcement was not ready to name this newest victim as one belonging to BTK, but they soon realized it was his handiwork. Strangulation was his preferred method and the bruising on her neck revealed she was strangled to death. Additionally, she was found with her legs and arms tied, which was another indicator that the BTK Killer of Wichita, Kansas had struck again.

# Chapter 11:

## His Final Murders

The BTK Killer had spent nearly a decade killing by the time he murdered Marine Hedge in April of 1985. A year later, he would strike again leaving law enforcement scrambling to find answers.

In September of 1986, Rader began stalking his next victim, Vicki Wegerle, who was 28-years-old. Her home address was 2404 West 13th Street North, Wichita, just nine miles away from the home of Rader's previous victim.

He needed a new way to excite himself and devised the plan of entering her home as a telephone repair man. Rader drove to her home in his own car and knocked on her front door. When she answered, he told her he was a telephone repairman and that he needed to check her phone lines. She allowed him into her home not realizing he was the BTK Killer.

She showed Rader where the phone was and he pretended to check the phone with a made-up gadget he invented. When Vicki Wegerle turned her back to Rader, he quickly pulled out his gun and told her to stop moving. Upon doing so, Vicki turned around and realized he was not a repairman. She realized she was in grave danger.

He told her to go to the bedroom where he then tied her up. However, she broke the bond he tied around her hands and they started fighting. After a few moments of fighting, Rader regained control of his victim and proceeded to strangle her. In Rader's own words he recollected, "I finally got the hand on her and I got a nylon sock and started strangling her."

He wrapped the sock around her neck and pulled tightly. Rader later remarked, "I finally gained on her and put her down and I thought she was dead, but apparently, she wasn't."

After Rader finished strangling her, he rearranged her clothes and took some pictures of her dying body. After he had his pictures, he quickly packed up his things; since he knew her husband would be home soon. He finished packing his belongings, grabbed her car keys, and drove away in her car. The paramedics arrived shortly after Rader had left, but failed in their attempts to revive her. Vicki died on September 16, 1986.

Rader disappeared again after strangling Vicki Wegerle. Law enforcement were stunned and still had no leads or evidence that would indicate the identity of the killer. Rader vanished and began playing the part of "God" once more by becoming invisible. He could watch the terror he caused in Wichita from the comfort of his own home with his family. They were terrified that the BTK Killer would come to their home and strangle them.

Rader reassured them they were safe and he probably found it amusing since he could control his own family's fate. Rader's wife and children had no idea he had been sneaking away to strangle people nor did they know anything of his sexual fantasies. However, Rader's silence would not last forever.

After five long years, he decided to strike again on January 19, 1991 by strangling 62-year-old Dolores Davis in her home in the middle of the night. The best description of the strangulation of Dolores Davis is from Rader's own words.

Rader said:

> On that particular day, I had some commitments. I left those, went to one place changed my clothes, went to another place, parked my car, finally made arrangements on my hit kit, changed my clothes and then walked to that residence. After spending some time at that residence —it was very cold that night— I had reservations about going in but I had cased the place before and I really couldn't figure out how to get in and she was in the house so I finally just selected a concrete block and threw it through the plate glass window...I just went in.
>
> She came out of the bedroom and thought that a car had hit her house and I told her, I used the ruse of being wanted; I was on the run. I needed food, car, warmth...I handcuffed her and kind of talked to her —told her that I would like to get some food, get her keys to her car. Kind of rest assured, talked with her a little bit, calmed her down a little bit...Then I went back and removed her handcuffs and tied her up and then, eventually, strangled her.

Rader altered from his normal method and strangled Dolores with her own pantyhose. After she died, he rolled her up in a blanket and shoved her in the trunk of her car. Somewhere in the mix of things, Rader realized he had lost his gun and went back into the home to find it. The gun had fallen out of his holster when he broke the window with the cinderblock and found it laying in the glass. He picked it up and got back into the car to drive to leave her body under a bridge. In Rader's own words, "I drove up northeast of Sedgwick County and dropped her off underneath a bridge." Her body would later be discovered near the river.

# Chapter 12:

## "Cereal" Killer

After his final murder, the BTK Killer disappeared again. Investigators were stunned and still had no solid leads or evidence that pointed to the identity of the BTK Killer. With no evidence to look to, and no way of knowing when he would strike next, investigators were forced to wait for the BTK Killer to make another move in hopes that he would leave some type of clue behind.

However, the BTK Killer vanished; and this time for good or so it would seem. He was silent for so long that most believed he had died from old age. After all, these killings began during the 1970s and continued until his final murder in 1991. By this time, the BTK Killer, whoever he was, must have been an old man, at least this was the belief among investigators.

By 2004, the BTK Killer case was cold even after many different lead investigators had worked on it. After all, the same evidence had been reanalyzed countless times by different people over the past three decades. Investigators simply made a small task forced that managed the cold case with the hope that he might reappear.

However, in the same year the case went cold, the BTK Killer suddenly reappeared. There was a book written about the BTK Killer and was announced to be published in 2005. The invisible man behind the BTK Killer could not keep silent once he learned of the book. In 2004, a letter was sent to the local new station, The Wichita Eagle, and the return address had the name, "Bill Thomas Killman."

The letter contained pictures of the body of Vicki dying in her home and a photocopy of her driver's license. Vicki had still been alive when paramedics arrived, so no pictures of her were taken at the scene. This proved that whoever sent the letter was, in fact, at the crime scene before investigators arrived in September of 1986.

The initials of the name, "Bill Thomas Killman," were unmistakably "BTK", which led the news team to contact police since they believed the letter was sent by the BTK Killer.

Immediately, newspapers began to publish the headlining story as the BTK Killer had returned. A town once filled with panic had now returned to the same familiar feeling. Those who knew of the BTK Killer no longer felt safe in their homes because they knew he could sneak in and strangle them to death.

Still, the BTK Killer continued to send messages to news stations and law enforcement. He would send them pictures of victims he had killed, showing how he moved their bodies after killing them to take his pictures of their bondage. He even took new pictures to send the clear message to investigators that the BTK Killer had returned.

In one instance, he went as far as to take a picture of a Barbie doll and a drainage pipe while having a noose attached to the neck of the Barbie doll and pipe; depicting the murder scene of Josie Otero. He wrote a puzzle story about the BTK Killer's "career" and even put chapter titles in it. Rader left cereal boxes for law enforcement to find because the word "cereal" sounds like "serial" killer.

No one knew when the BTK Killer would strike again and the city began to panic.

However, law enforcement realized that the problem they had the last time was the BTK Killer did not talk to them enough to trace him. Their method this time was to keep him talking by feeding his ego. They began to hold press conferences that were designed to specifically speak to the serial killer. Their broadcasting efforts were soon gratified as the BTK Killer began to talk. This led to investigators trapping the BTK and finally revealing his identity as Dennis Rader, the "family man" who was president of Christ Lutheran Church in Wichita, Kansas.

The capture of Dennis Rader was different than most serial killers. The BTK Killer began to trust investigators after he started communicating with them.

The world of investigation was different than what it was in the 1970s when Rader began killing. Investigators now had better technology and new ways of tracing lines of communication. When Rader continued communication with investigators, he wanted to type things out on his computer and sent it to them on a floppy disk. He asked investigators if there was a way to trace the disk. Of course, they lied to him.

When he dropped the floppy disk in the desired location, investigators traced it back to a church in Wichita, Kansas. At first, they thought it might have been a sick joke, but they found a name attached to the file. The name attached was "Dennis" and was the first time they had a name associated with the BTK Killer.

Naturally, they checked the name to see who it belonged to. Since the floppy disk came from a church, the person who sent it must be associated with the church. Investigators did a simple Google search and found the name "Dennis Rader." He was listed as the president of the church, Christ Lutheran Church.

The floppy disk gave investigators a name and address, but it was not enough to prove Dennis Rader was the BTK Killer. It was just circumstantial evidence.

Investigators needed solid evidence to prove Dennis Rader was the BTK, but they had no way of obtaining evidence. That is, of course, until investigators found the missing piece to their puzzle when Rader began to play games with them.

Rader started leaving messages in boxes of cereal to emphasize that he was in fact a serial killer. He took great joy in this humor and continued to play games with investigators. However, Rader tossed a box of cereal in the back of someone's pickup truck and the person threw it in the trash. After days with no response, Rader asked about his message. Investigators eventually found the box and retrieved the message.

The important factor to investigators was not the message in the box, but the location in which Rader placed the box in the truck. He placed it in the truck in the parking lot of a home improvement store and the security cameras recorded the make and model of his car. While they could not see his face, they knew the type of car he drove.

Investigators went by Dennis Rader's home, just out of sheer curiosity, and found the same car sitting in his driveway. They knew they had identified the BTK Killer, but still did not have enough evidence to convict him.

By 2004, new scientific technology made it possible to create a DNA profile. Investigators reevaluated Rader's semen sample taken from the crime scenes and created a DNA profile. However, his profile was useless because they did not have a person to match it with.

When detectives found the name, address and car, they decided to check the DNA of Dennis Rader's daughter, Kerri Rawson, to see if it was a family match to the semen the BTK had left at the crime scenes. After waiting patiently, the results revealed the truth; the Kerri Rawson's father was the BTK Killer.

Detectives arrested Dennis Rader for the murders committed in Wichita, Kansas between 1974 and 1991.

After Rader was taken into custody, he was interrogated by investigators for thirty hours. Three hours into the interrogation, Rader cracked by admitting he was the BTK Killer and began to tell them everything he could remember. Shortly after his interrogation, his trial began where he confessed to Judge Gregory Waller all the murders he had committed. His confession was cold and emotionless and describes the crimes and murder scenes in detail.

After hearing the confession of Dennis Rader, Judge Gregory Waller asked Rader a simple question:

> Judge: "So, all of these instances, these 10 counts, occurred because you wanted to fulfill a sexual fantasy. Is that correct?"
>
> Rader: "Yes, uh-huh."

# Chapter 13:

## The Clueless Family?

Paula Rader was married to the BTK Killer for 34 years. She was granted a divorce after he was arrested. She later changed her name and dropped off the radar. Many people still wonder if she really had no idea she was married to a serial killer.

Obviously the BTK Killer was quite good at living a double life, but there were obvious signs something was off.

During the height of the media hype and fear around him, Paula found a poem her husband had written. It was a rough draft of the "Shirleylocks, Shirleylocks" poem. When she questioned him, her husband claimed he was writing it for a class for school. To be fair, he was studying criminal justice, but it is doubtful that any teacher would demand their students write about a recent murder from the eyes of a serial killer.

Paula let it slide.

Local new stations regularly published letters written by the BTK Killer. At one point, Paula picked up a letter her husband was writing to one of his brothers and even commented that he wrote just like the BTK Killer.

Again, Paula let it slide.

Perhaps the most questionable thing was, however, recordings. The BTK Killer had called the police himself to inform them of one of his murders. This call was recorded. It was played again and again on the news. Somehow, Paula didn't recognize her own husband's voice.

So, was Paula aware, or was she merely turning a blind eye? That I will leave for to you to decide.

# Conclusion:

# How The BTK Story Ends

After Dennis Rader confessed and pleaded guilty to strangling ten people in Wichita, Kansas he was sentenced to served consecutive life sentences —a minimum of 175 years. Rader was 60-years-old when he was captured and is 72-years-old at the publication of this book. He will undoubtedly spend the remainder of his life in prison unless he somehow manages to escape.

The BTK Killer felt like there was a monster living inside of him and he finally lost control of it in January of 1974. After his capture, he described this monster as a demon living inside of him. He claims to have had no control over his actions and believes something else caused him to strangle his victims.

While Rader may have been born into a nice family, and had a family of his own, he tortured other families by strangling people to death for his own sexual gratification. For Rader, remorse was an unnecessary emotion. The thought of taking life with his bare hands made his heart thump and his brain tick.

Rader's act of strangulation led to more intense methods after the killing of the Otero family. Once he felt comfortable killing, he began to strangle his victims again and again before letting them finally die. He would strangle his victims until the point of death and then let them regain their breath so he could strangle them again. In the mist of his victim's recovery, he would whisper in their ear, "I am BTK."

He lived a double life for more than thirty years and his wife and children claimed they knew nothing of the ten people he murdered until he was captured in 2005. On the outside, he was Dennis Rader, the family man who lived in a good community and worked full-time. He had never been to jail or had any trouble with the law. On the inside, he was an overconfident, cold-blooded murderer who killed because he thought he could get away with anything.

# Sources

Anderson, P. (2014, October 6). "Dennis Rader — aka the 'BTK Killer' — wanted his nickname on the list of the world's worst serial killers". Retrieved from http://www.heraldsun.com.au/news/law-order/true-crime-scene/dennis-rader-aka-the-btk-killer-wanted-his-nickname-on-the-list-of-the-worlds-worst-serial-killers/news-story/10dc3c703a5fc3408b26f65021bf6638

ABC News. (2005, February 25). "Neighbor: I Watched BTK Suspect Shoot Dog". Retrieved from http://abcnews.go.com/GMA/LegalCenter/story?id=535740&page=1

Bardsley, M., Bell, R., Lohr, D. (2008, May 29). "The BTK Story". Retrieved from https://web.archive.org/web/20080529005912/http://www.trutv.com/library/crime/serial_killers/unsolved/btk/13.html

Beattie, R. (2005). *Nightmare in Wichita: The Hunt For The BTK Strangler*

Biography.com Editors. (2017, May 24). Dennis Rader Biography.com. Retrieved from https://www.biography.com/people/dennis-rader-241487

"BTK: 'I took her to the basement and...hung her' , Suspect Dennis Rader details killings in court". (2005, June 27). Retrieved from http://www.cnn.com/2005/LAW/06/27/rader.transcript/

"BTK sentenced to 10 life terms, Victims' families confront confessed serial murderer". (2005, August 18). Retrieved from http://www.cnn.com/2005/LAW/08/18/btk.killings/


"'BTK' serial killer caught". (2005, February 27). Retrieved from http://www.theage.com.au/news/World/BTK-serial-killer-caught/2005/02/27/1109439444107.html


"BTK serial killer Dennis Rader planned to murder 11th victim". (2016, August 19). Retrieved from http://www.nydailynews.com/news/crime/btk-serial-killer-dennis-rader-planned-murder-11th-victim-article-1.2758433


"BTK Strangler resurfaces after 25 years". (2004, March 29). Retrieved from http://www.scotsman.com/news/world/btk-strangler-resurfaces-after-25-years-1-519136


Buselt, L. (2005, March 03). "Park City Council dismisses Rader". Retrieved from https://web.archive.org/web/20050305052051/http://www.kansas.com/mld/kansas/news/special_packages/btk/11037860.htm


"City's 'BTK Strangler' claims he's killed 7". (1978). Retrieved from http://www.kansas.com/news/special-reports/btk/article1003859.html


Crawford, M. I. "Profile of a Serial Killer: Dennis Rader, the BTK Strangler". Retrieved from https://owlcation.com/social-sciences/Profile-of-a-Serial-Killer-Part-5-Dennis-Rader-The-BTK-Killer

Crime Feed Staff. (2015, November 30). "6 SERIAL KILLER QUOTES THAT WILL SEND CHILLS DOWN YOUR SPINE". Retrieved from http://crimefeed.com/2015/11/excuse-6-horrific-serial-killer-quotes/

"Dennis Lynn Rader". Murderpedia. Retrieved from http://murderpedia.org/male.R/r/rader-dennis-dolores-davis.htm

http://murderpedia.org/male.R/r/rader-dennis.htm

"Dennis Rader". Criminalminds. Retrieved from http://criminalminds.wikia.com/wiki/Dennis_Rader

Dennis Rader (BTK Killer). (2017). The Famous People website. Retrieved from //www.thefamouspeople.com/profiles/dennis-rader-btk-killer-29880.php

"DENNIS RADER - BTK KILLER - A BIOGRAPHY". Retrieved from http://dennisraderbtk.blogspot.com/

Dodd, J., Douglas, J. (2008). *Inside the Mind of BTK: The True Story Behind the Thirty-Year Hunt for the Notorious Wichita Serial Killer*.

"Four in Wichita family found slain at home". (1974). Retrieved from http://www.kansas.com/news/special-reports/btk/article1003854.html

Grant, S. (2013, March 19). "10 Baffling Wives of Serial Killers". Retrieved from https://listverse.com/2013/03/19/10-baffling-wives-of-serial-killers/

Hegeman, R. (2004, August 27). "Police: '79 poem was written by BTK killer". Retrieved from http://cjonline.com/stories/082704/kan_btkpoem.shtml

Hickey, E. W. (2012). *Serial Murderers and their Victims*.

McClellan, Janet (2010, May 18). *Erotophonophilia: Investigating Lust Murder*.

McDonnell, D. A., Symon, E. V. (2012, April 29). "5 Supposedly Badass Criminals Caught in Embarrassing Ways". Retrieved from http://www.cracked.com/article_19779_5-supposedly-badass-criminals-caught-in-embarrassing-ways.html

Meadows, B. (2005, March 21). "The BTK Case: the Killer Unmasked?". Retrieved from http://people.com/archive/the-btk-case-the-killer-unmasked-vol-63-no-11/

Murphy, H. (2016, September 12). "BTK Serial Killer: What We Learned From Confessional New Book". Retrieved from http://www.rollingstone.com/culture/news/btk-serial-killer-inside-confessional-new-book-w439143

Newton, Michael (2000) "The Encyclopedia of Serial Killers". Checkmark Books. New York: New York.

"Paula and Dennis Raders' divorce granted". (2005, July 27). Retrieved from http://www.kansas.com/news/special-reports/btk/article1003760.html

"Police destroy 1,326 DNA samples taken in BTK investigation". (2006, May 31). Retrieved from https://usatoday30.usatoday.com/news/nation/2006-05-31-DNA-BTK_x.htm

Rachels, D. (2012). "Pulp Poem of the Week". Retrieved from http://noirboiled.blogspot.com/2012/09/pulp-poem-of-week.html

Rader, D. "OH! DEATH TO NANCY". Retrieved from https://web.archive.org/web/20060603033530/http://www.wichitagov.org/NR/rdonlyres/909034E1-C202-4844-91E2-8231E12AFEFE/0/OhDeathtoNancy.pdf

Reitwiesner, W. A. "Ancestry of Dennis Rader". Retrieved from http://www.wargs.com/other/rader.html

"Son of BTK victim still haunted: Man says he witnessed mother's slaying as a 5-year-old". (2005, March 2). Retrieved from http://edition.cnn.com/2005/LAW/03/01/btk.relford/

Sutton, C. (2017, April 3). "The Macdonald triad: Theory on childhood signs of a future serial killer". Retrieved from http://www.news.com.au/national/crime/the-macdonald-triad-theory-on-childhood-signs-of-a-future-serial-killer/news-story/ff8efd1221e88610abcc349d5725d5bc

Sylvester, R. (2005, August 18). "Investigators tell of grisly crimes, Rader's delight". Retrieved from http://www.kansas.com/news/special-reports/btk/article1003774.html


Vigliotti, J. (2015, March 17). "10 Things You Never Knew About The BTK Killer". Retrieved from http://listverse.com/2015/03/17/10-things-you-never-knew-about-the-btk-killer/


Wenzl, Roy; Potter, Tim; Laviana, Hurst; Kelly, L. (2008, May 27). *Bind, Torture, Kill: The Inside Story of BTK, the Serial Killer Next Door.*


Wenzl, R. (2014, September 25). "BTK's daughter: Stephen King 'exploiting my father's 10 victims and their families' with movie". Retrieved from http://www.kansas.com/news/special-reports/btk/article2251870.html


Wenzl, R. (2015, February 21). "When your father is the BTK serial killer, forgiveness is not tidy". Retrieved from http://www.kansas.com/news/special-reports/btk/article10809929.html

Printed in Great Britain
by Amazon